Frida Kahlo

A Selective Annotated Bibliography of

Dissertations and Theses

Louis V. Allene

Allene, Louis V.

Frida Kahlo: A selective annotated bibliography of dissertations and theses/Louis V. Allene

p. cm.

1. Kahlo, Frida, 1907-1954 -- Criticism and Interpretation. 2. Magic Realism. I. Title.

ND 259 .K33
759

ISBN-10 1511646470
ISBN-13 978-1511646475

Cover - The Blue House, Frida Kahlo's Home

Other titles by Louis V. Allene

Juan Rulfo: A selective annotated bibliography of dissertations and theses

Octavio Paz: A selective annotated bibliography of dissertations and theses

Gabriel Garcia Marquez: A selective annotated bibliography of dissertations and theses

Carlos Fuentes: A selective annotated bibliography of dissertations and theses

Jorge Luis Borges: A selective annotated bibliography of dissertations and theses

Isabel Allende A selective annotated bibliography of dissertations and theses

Jose Donoso: A selective annotated bibliography of dissertations and theses

Frida Kahlo A selective annotated bibliography of dissertations and theses

Diego Rivera: A selective annotated bibliography of dissertations and theses

Magic Realism: A selective annotated bibliography of dissertations and theses

Table of Contents

1.)   **Arellano, C.**

The importance of the Xoloitzcuintli in Mexican history and in the works of Diego Rivera and Frida Kahlo.

M.A. thesis, California State University, Los Angeles. 2012.

The image of the Mexican hairless dog, or Xoloitzcuintli, has famously been immortalized in Diego Rivera's murals and in the paintings of Frida Kahlo. The Xoloitzcuintli has become part of a rich Mexican history. The purpose of this study is to place the dog in Mexican history, trace it back before the Spanish colonization, and reevaluate the role of the Xoloitzcuintli in the Aztec civilization. This would be done in order to understand the impact that this animal had in its society and why it motivated 20th century artists to depict it in their works. [Author Abstract]

2.) **Baizer, G. S.**

Wearing her emotions on her sleeve: Costuming Frida Kahlo's self-portraits.

M.F.A. thesis, California State University, Long Beach. 2005.

This project report focuses on Frida Kahlo's unique form of costume expression, as seen in her self-portraits. Through the examination of documents, texts, photographs, and artwork, it is apparent that in her self-portraits, Frida masked her persona behind a stoic self-image using costume, color, and symbolic imagery to unmask her inner turmoil. Frida's artwork and costume dissolved the distinction between her internal and external worlds; therefore, her personal and artistic identities are inseparable. The American premiere of Dreams of a Sunday Afternoon, written by playwright Maritza Nunez, was produced by the California Repertory Theatre at California State University, Long Beach, in February,

2004. My costume design for this production was the visual interpretation of Frida Kahlo's vast reservoir of symbolic imagery and inner turmoil as seen in her self-portraits. [Author Abstract]

3.) **Bartolone, R. F.**

Re-thinking the language of pain in the works of Marguerite Duras and Frida Kahlo. Ph.D. dissertation, The University of North Carolina at Chapel Hill. 2006.

This dissertation is a cross-cultural examination of the creation and the sociocultural implications of the languages of pain in the works of French author, Marguerite Duras and Mexican painter, Frida Kahlo. Recent studies have determined that discursive communication is insufficient in expressing one's pain. In particular, Elaine Scarry maintains that pain destroys language and that its victims must rely on the vocabulary of other cultural spheres in order to express their pain. The problem is that neither Scarry nor any other Western pain scholar can provide an alternative to discursive language to express pain. This study claims that both artists must work beyond their own cultural registers in order to give their pain a language. In the process of expressing their suffering, Duras and Kahlo subvert traditional literary and artistic conventions. Through challenging literary and artistic forms, they begin to re-think and ultimately re-define the way their readers and viewers understand feminine subjectivity, colonial and wartime occupation, personal tragedy, the female body, Christianity and Western hegemony. [Author Abstract]

4.)   **Beck, E. T.**
Physical illness, psychological woundedness and the healing power of art in the life and work of Franz Kafka and Frida Kahlo.
Ph.D. dissertation, Fielding Graduate Institute. 2004.

This dissertation is a comparative case study focusing on the life and work of Franz Kafka and Frida Kahlo, with special attention to the physical illness and psychological woundedness that permeated their lives and which they transmuted into the images of their art. Both artists depicted violence and bodily injury in their work, referencing wounds that were "unsayable" in life and could only be symbolized in art. For both, art served to express and assuage the psychological experience of these wounds within "the holding environment of the artistic endeavor." This narrative inquiry incorporates constructivist,

phenomenological, hermenuetic, feminist,

and psychoanalytic perspectives, especially object relations and self psychology. It is based on primary literary and visual texts as well as secondary sources, including standard biographies of these artists. From the vast body of primary material, selections were chosen based for their pertinence to the themes of "wounds, blood and woundings." This study is also informed by Gruber's "Evolving Systems Approach" to the study of creative individuals and his conceptual categories of "ensembles of metaphors" and "networks of enterprise." The dissertation provides the cultural, historical, and personal contexts for these artists' life and work upon which later interpretations are based and explores the motivational factors that allowed these artists to make reparative use of creative processes in spite of chronic physical illness and psychic anguish. Several chapters elaborate the kinds of wounds to the self that Kafka and Kahlo grappled with in their relationships and which they expressively tried to heal through the holding environment of their art. All chapters are comparative except for one that is dedicated entirely to Kahlo because it explores an ensemble of gender specific images which suggest that Kahlo may have been expressing in her art an otherwise "unspeakable" history of sexual abuse. The final chapters interrogate the function of the blood and wounds that mark these artists' work and explore the psychological mechanisms through which healing may have taken place. The dissertation concludes that the process of producing art may have worked therapeutically for Kafka and Kahlo, enabling them to break through and enliven the "psychic deadness" that plagued them. [Author Abstract]

5.)   **Beer, M. M.**

Modern Mexican art and history: The art of Diego Rivera and Frida Kahlo.

M.A. thesis, California State University, Dominguez Hills. 1994.

The research contained herein is the result of searching local and university libraries for formerly published research, and will thoroughly examine and discuss particular art works by both Diego Rivera and Frida Kahlo. In addition to the detailed analysis of their respective workmanship, the relevant history and culture of the time period in which they lived will be documented and clarified. Likewise, the societal impact and importance of their specific works will also be studied. Furthermore, the influence of their craft will be considered. The cultural, social and historical forces that brought about their masterpieces will be discussed including the dominant role that politics played in shaping their distinctive works. Finally, the personal significance of their creations will be determined for each artist respectively. [Author Abstract]

6.)   **Brown, A. H.**

A psychoanalytic study of art: The work of Frida Kahlo.

Psy.D. dissertation, The Wright Institute. 2006.

This study draws upon the literature of psychoanalytic theory, formal art analysis, and the life and work of Frida Kahlo to illustrate the proposed process of the interpretation of the unconscious through art. This study differs from a

psychobiographical approach in that it utilizes a distinct methodology that includes examining Kahlo's paintings through a formal art analysis. Subsequently, the outcome of the formal analysis will be integrated with autobiographical, biographical, social, political, cultural, and scholarship information, and analyzed through an object relations lens. This examination will illuminate psychological constructs, such as splitting, projection and introjection using a combined approach: the formal art analysis with the psychoanalytic study of the artist. The proposed methodology broadens the interpretive techniques of both psychoanalytic and art-historical discussions of paintings and offers an alternative for psychoanalytic studies in art, suggesting a methodology that can broaden the interpretive techniques of both psychoanalytic and art-historical discussions of painting. On a large scale, this study examines how creative work reflects unconscious psychic life, and how the artistic endeavor can be a tool to better illuminate the unconscious. [Author Abstract]

7.)   **Crary-Ortega, L.**

Representations of the self: Problems of image and identity in the self-portraits of Frida Kahlo.

Ph.D. dissertation, University of Pittsburgh. 1997.

Frida Kahlo's face has come to represent struggle; struggle against physical adversity and the emotional vicissitudes of having an unfaithful husband; struggle to carve out an individual identity from the mass of imposed cultural and societal norms; the struggle to be recognized as an artist as a woman in a masculinist world. Kahlo's self-portraits present a compelling body of work to examine for the complicated ways in which individual identity is socially constructed of convergent factors of nationality, gender, class, ethnicity and race. This dissertation analyzes the artist's self-portraits to show how her work calls into question ideas of an innate, fixed self, and concomitant terms like 'authenticity' and 'truth' when applied to interpretations of life and art. These ideas are shown instead to be more fluid, leading to more possible interpretations of Kahlo's work than the predominantly biographical approach taken by most writers. The profusion of photographs of Kahlo in her many guises contributes to the tendency to want her art to speak for her. The simplicity that this gives to the entire interpretive enterprise speaks for a desire to find the single objective truth of a painting, a problematic approach that has led to a suppression of many interpretations made possible by Kahlo's self-portraits. This dissertation argues that construction of meaning occurs not only when an art work is produced, but each time the work is viewed and interpreted. Frida Kahlo's art has become an important part of women's art history and popular culture. The popularity of her art indicates that it helps to fulfill some of the needs and desires of those who interpret Kahlo and her art. It is crucial to return to Kahlo's paintings themselves to examine how she laid the groundwork for the strong identification with her that is experienced by so many different groups of people. [Author Abstract]

8.)   **Deffebach, N.**

Images of plants in the art of Maria Izquierdo, Frida Kahlo, and Leonora Carrington: Gender, identity, and spirituality in the context of modern Mexico.

Ph.D. dissertation, The University of Texas at Austin. 2000.

This study examines images of plants in the work of María Izquierdo, Frida Kahlo, and Leonora Carrington. The selection of these artists is based on the prevalence and significance of plants in their paintings and their association with three separate artistic circles in postrevolutionary and mid-twentieth century Mexico that held conflicting views about the function of art. Because plants grow nearly everywhere and are part of our daily lives, their appearance in the work of Izquierdo, Kahlo, and Carrington may seem innocuous, innocent, mere background to the main event. Nothing could be further from the truth. Beyond the iconographic significance of plants--which is often crucial for the understanding of individual works--the vegetation is a vehicle for introducing gender issues. And gender is invariably intertwined with other issues. At stake is the construction of women, the invention of nature, the identity of the Mexican nation, and the question of who is allowed interpretive power. Botanical imagery is approached as a way of focusing on themes that are important to the three artists, thus shifting the focus to their ideas and away from their personal lives. Key issues include how they used images of plants to link themselves symbolically to locations, legacies, and social conditions. The study considers the political implications of these linkages, and how the imagery participated in and resisted aspects of artistic and nationalistic discourses. Decades before "the personal is political" became a slogan of the women's liberation movement, Izquierdo, Kahlo, and Carrington used the principle to convert domestic space and the kitchen garden into legitimate subjects and to turn the still life genre on its head. At a time and place where the dominant discourse promoted heroes and revolution, the three artists inscribed female experience into artistic discourse by inventing strong female personages who are closely linked to the natural environment and the vegetal realm. [Author Abstract]

9.) **Delgado, M.**

The female grotesque in the works of Gabriel Garcia Marquez, Isabel Allende, and Frida Kahlo.

Ph.D. dissertation, The University of Texas at Dallas. 2010.

If one summarizes the characteristics of the "grotesque," one finds it is extreme, exaggerated, extravagant, ridiculous, estranged, abnormal, surreal, subversive, tragic, comic, or beautiful. There is a close connection between the grotesque and women: Starting with their own bodies, women are associated with elements of the grotesque such as the uncanny, the extravagant, the witch, and the fatal devouring female, among others. Some scholars consider that there is a close relationship between a grotesque female body and a political body of a nation, e.g., Mary Russo in The Female Grotesque (1986) connects the essence of the grotesque with the role of women as leaders who fight for positive changes in their societies. Upon analyzing the essence of the grotesque, it is easy to see that the Latin American continent has become a grotesque world, for it is estranged, alienated, and dominated and manipulated by powerful systems, and women are directly affected by this phenomenon. For many centuries, since the time of the conquest of Latin America, the majority of women have been placed in secondary positions: housewives, mothers, nuns, servants, or just underpaid laborers. Traditional and official institutions have contributed to the discrimination, exploitation, and oppression of women and have promoted and encouraged a conduct of machismo. I argue that as a response to this phenomenon, many writers, painters, and other intellectuals have used the grotesque as a way of protest against historical acts of oppression, discrimination, and alienation of women. For instance, writers Gabriel García

Márquez and Isabel Allende depict extreme situations in their narratives and also propose solutions to work on behalf of all women. In visual arts, artists create grotesque symbols through unconventional paintings in order to defeat oppressive regimes. Mexican painter Frida Kahlo is an example of this kind of expression. Projecting her own image in a variety of depictions, Kahlo creates a new dimension of social protest against women's discrimination. [Author Abstract]

10.)   **Duncan, M. A.**

A psychobiography of Frida Kahlo.

Ph.D. dissertation, Adelphi University, The Institute of Advanced Psychological Studies. 1995.

Psychobiographical methodology was used to explore the life and work of the Mexican painter Frida Kahlo. Multiple levels of analysis were incorporated in this study. First, the historical and cultural context of Mexico during the early 20th century was investigated. Particular attention was given to the artistic traditions and the complex role of women which influenced Kahlo. Second, biographical data about the artist, including the intricacies of her family background and a detailed developmental history, was examined. Finally, the interior life of the artist was explored through the detailed study of a significant number of her highly autobiographical paintings, particularly her self-portraits. Psychological formulations were based upon British object relations theory, particularly the work of Melanie Klein and her proponents. The psychoanalytic perspective enabled a deeper exploration of the vast reservoir of unconscious material which are expressed through Kahlo's vivid imagery and individualistic use of formal elements. The complex synthesis of historical, cultural, biographical, and psychological data for the study of Kahlo's life and art, has facilitated an enriched and variegated understanding of Kahlo the individual. At a broader level, the analysis of Kahlo the individual is a step towards shedding light on a heretofore understudied group: The woman artist. This psychobiographical study stands as one of the few in-depth explorations of a woman artist. [Author Abstract]

11.)   **Fernandez, L. B.**

An exploration and analysis of the sociological content in the art of Frida Kahlo: Mexican ethnic and cultural identity, feminism, the struggle of the disable and her political ideology.

M.A. thesis, California State University, Dominguez Hills. 2001.

Generally Frida Kahlo has been regarded as a symbol of beauty, of strength in adversity, and a kind of phoenix that through art rises from the ashes of her life experience. Little emphasis has been placed on her sociological views and political activism. Frida used images of her own body and face to express her ideas, as a result of this some art critics and historians have believed her art to be strictly personal. However, her physical self was at the crossroads between her internal life and her external life, in other words it was the place where psychology and sociology met.

Therefore, the statements that Frida made using depictions of her physical self were also statements about society at large. The themes of Mexican ethnic and cultural identity, Marxism, feminism and the struggle of the sick and disabled are clearly present in her paintings. This research is dedicated to exploring and analyzing the sociological content of Frida Kahlo's artistic expression by focussing on four of her striking paintings: A Few Little Pricks, 1935, My Nurse and I, 1937, Tree of Hope, Keep Firm, 1946, and Marxism Will Give Health to the Sick, 1954. [Author Abstract]

12.)   **Hauptman, T. L.**

Federico Garcia Lorca's notion of duende in the paintings of Frida Kahlo and the poetry of Pablo Neruda: Toward a poetics of synthesis. Ph.D. dissertation, Ohio University. 1997.

"Federico Garcia Lorca's Notion Of Duende In The Paintings Of Frida Kahlo And The Poetry of Pablo Neruda" illuminates Lorca's notion of duende as an artistic principle in particular paintings of Frida Kahlo and specific poems of Pablo Neruda. Duende's power of transformation ultimately juxtaposes Kahlo and Neruda in a synthesized, metapoetic correspondence. Surrealism, Mexicanidad, and Modernism are investigated as well as retablo, ex-voto, cante jondo, deep song, traditional modes, and movements. Spiritual autobiographies commingle historically, culturally, and contextually as synaesthethic visual/verbal/musical elements move in space-time. Kahlo's paintings and Neruda's poems, duende-driven, are analyzed for their intrinsic deep sound and tragic elements that paradoxically turn life to death/death to life within a Mexican and Chilean political and cultural perspective. This dissertation demonstrates the correspondence between Kahlo's paintings and Neruda's poems based upon a commingling of the concept of duende and surrealist techniques and aims. Internal structure and intertextuality are investigated in a series of interrelated questions while focusing on interpenetration and interaction between Kahlo's paintings and Neruda's poems. The nature of surrealist vision, Mexicanidad, and Latin American poetics creates a bridge between the arts of Kahlo and Neruda illumined and defined by Lorca's notion of duende. [Author Abstract]

13.)   **Herrera, H.**
Frida Kahlo: Her life, her art.
Ph.D. dissertation, City University of New York. 1981.

The Mexican painter Frida Kahlo (1908-1954) is already something of a cult figure in her native Mexico. Her legendary stature is in part due to her marriage to the renowned muralist Diego Rivera, in part to her extraordinary personality and in part to her pursuit of a career in painting despite being a partial cripple. If Kahlo's value as an artist has long been recognized in Mexico, however, it is still not well known in the United States. Nonetheless, there seems to be a growing interest in her work here, mainly because her art speaks directly and vividly about the most private facets of specifically female experience. Kahlo's life and art are so intimately connected that one cannot be understood without the other. My central concern has been to unravel the various levels of meaning in Frida Kahlo's highly personal imagery and to relate formal and iconographic analysis to events in Kahlo's life and to her feelings about those events. To do this I have drawn upon Kahlo's writings--among them her letters and her diary--and upon over one hundred interviews that I conducted in Mexico, France and the U.S. However distanced by fantasy and by mock-naive style, Kahlo's paintings--almost all of them self portraits -- record an invalid's quest for strength through direct confrontation with her own painful reality. She painted herself weeping, for example, split open in surgery, hemorrhaging during a miscarriage and pierced by arrows, thorns and nails. She painted, also, the joys and sorrows of being Rivera's wife. In her art and in her life, Frida Kahlo stressed her Mexican identity. She portrayed herself in the Mexican costumes she wore daily; the primary sources for her art were Mexican pre-Columbian, Colonial and popular art. But

Kahlo was a sophisticated painter, one whose art bespeaks her knowledge of Surrealism, European modernism and the work of her Mexican contemporaries. She thus chose a primitivistic approach for complex reasons. She lived in a cultured and varied milieu (both in Mexico and the U.S. where she and Rivera spent several years). The leftist politics she shared with her husband and her involvement in the ferment of Mexican culture during the post-revolutionary year inform her work. Though she did not paint paeans to Mexico nor Marxist messages on public walls, she did paint emphatically Mexicanista images on small pieces of tin. Her art, amazingly enough, is not local or parochial: it focuses so narrowly, but so intensely on herself that it speaks to virtually all people. [Author Abstract]

14.)   **Hirschfeld, L. B.**

Painting the Spanish Civil War: Frida Kahlo's personal palette of political allegory.

M.A. thesis, Sarah Lawrence College. 2007.

Marking seventy years since the bombing of Guernica and the 100 centennial of the birth of Mexican painter Frida Kahlo (1907-1954), this study analyzes Kahlos' works as political allegories of the worldwide phenomenon of the Spanish Civil War. The artist's earliest influences begin this analysis---the graphic images of violence during the Mexican Revolution, her liberal education and rich European cultural stimuli, and the years in the United States as the young wife of Mexican muralist Diego Rivera. This thesis, as an effort to counteract the overwhelmingly sensationalist and simplistic treatment of the work of Frida Kahlo, addresses the shortcomings of previous historiography. A reading of Kahlo's Self Portrait Dedicated to Leon Trotsky provides insight into the political complexities, the causes of the conflict within Spain, and the international involvements of Communist Russia, Nazi Germany and Fascist Italy. Kahlo's reaction to the civilian casualties is seen in the paintings she presented at her Julien Levy Gallery Exhibition in New York on November 1938 in her efforts to rustle concern and assistance from an American public. As the war drew to a close, we see disillusionment and defeat in Kahlo's paintings as a result of her travels to Paris during this period. [Author Abstract]

15.)   **Loizou, M.**

"The Diary of Frida Kahlo": The genre, the book, the work.

M.A. thesis, University of Ottawa (Canada). 2002.

This study explores some fundamental aspects of The Diarv of Frida Kahlo. namely its classification as a diary, the impact of the prologues of the different versions on the diary's reception, and the various dialogues taking place within it and the rest of Kahlo's artistic production. The first part focuses on the classification of this work as a diary. The theoretical sources utilized to establish the characteristics of the diary genre are: Le journal intime by Beatrice Didier, and the scholarly article by Valerie Raoul, "Women and Diaries: Gender and Genre". This chapter demonstrates that there are certain aspects of Kahlo's diary that indeed correspond to the genre whereas other elements distance it from this classification.

In the second part of this study, the role and impact of the introduction and prefatory essays is examined. The basis of the analysis of the different prefaces is G6rard Genettes concept of the paratexte as elaborated in his book, Seuils. The English, French and German versions of the diary all share the same introduction by Carlos Fuentes and essay by Sarah Lowe. The Fuentes/Lowe preface presents the reader with a homogeneous approach to the diary which is shown to be related to the current "fridamania" phenomenon characterized primarily by its focus on Kahlo's life. The Spanish version omits Lowe's essay and includes three essays written by authors active in Mexico, Karen Cordero Reinman, Olivier Debroise and Graciela Martinez Zalce. Each of the essays interprets the diary differently. The various angles of interpretation are more congruous with the complexities found within the diary's pages as well as reflect the various facets of

Kahlo's artistic production. This preface provides Mexican readership with a more in-depth understanding of Kahlo's life and art. In the final part of the study an interpretation of Kahlo's diary is offered which focuses particularly on the notion of dialogue. The combination of modes, media, topics and icons found in the first entry are shown to be closely linked to Kahlo's artistic production. This third chapter proposes that Kahlo's diary is at times carefully constructed as is the case in the initial entry and slowly progresses to a much freer, less self-conscious form of expression. Certain media which is present both in her diary and in her painting is used to create different effects. This chapter demonstrates through a detailed descriptive analysis of the first entry that there exists a dialogue present on three different levels: within the diary itself, between the diary and Kahlo's artistic production and between the diary and Kahlo herself. [Author Abstract]

16.)   **Mayenzet, M. H.**

A historical approach to characterization: An analysis of Frida Kahlo in "Dreams of a Sunday Afternoon."

M.F.A.thesis, California State University, Long Beach. 2005.

This project report examines the exploratory and creative process necessary for the characterization of Frida Kahlo in Dreams of a Sunday Afternoon by Maritza Nunez, as performed by the California Repertory Company in the Edison Theatre, Long Beach, California, 21 February-13 March 2004. Historical research is an integral part of an actor's discovery and choices in the characterization of a role. Examining and exploring Frida Kahlo within the framework of historical research both informed and defined my characterization of Frida Kahlo in the symbolist and surreal production of Dreams of a Sunday Afternoon. In chapter 1 Frida Kahlo's life, history, ideology, and art are examined. Chapter 2 deals with the structure of the play, a historical approach to characterization, the rehearsal process, and the performance run of Dreams of a Sunday Afternoon. [Author Abstract]

17.)   **McCarthy, M. L.**

The flower beneath the stone: Uncovering D. H. Lawrence's natural affinities with Georgia O'Keeffe, Virginia Woolf, Frida Kahlo, and the mythic Laocoön.

Ph.D. dissertation, Northern Illinois University. 2013.

This dissertation considers elements of landscape in select works by D. H. Lawrence in relation to those of Virginia Woolf, Georgia O'Keeffe, and Frida Kahlo. It also reflects on the myth of Laocoön as it appears in his writings. The critical method employs an interart lens to: passages from Lawrence's novels, poetry, and prose; flower imagery in Woolf's first novel, The Voyage Out; paintings of flowers and trees by O'Keeffe; self-portraits and still lifes by Kahlo; and literary and sculptural adaptations of the myth of Laocoön. Excerpts from letters and essays, and examples of his artwork display his knowledge of, and passion for, botany (particularly flowers), painting, and sculpture. Studying the novels chronologically exposes startling changes in physical landscapes, the consciousnesses of characters that inhabit them, and the historical and cultural contexts in which they are set. When placed alongside works by Woolf, O'Keeffe, and Kahlo, Lawrence's depictions of elements of landscape reveal commonalities and divergences in matters of gender, sexuality, and male-female relationships. Additionally, in the process of reinterpreting the ancient myth of Laocoön, Lawrence creates a personal restoration of the sculptural Laocoön. [Author Abstract]

18.)   **Misemer, S. M.**

Cultural icons in Latin American theater: Studies of Frida Kahlo, Carlos Gardel, Eva Peron and Selena Quintanilla-Perez.

Ph.D. dissertation, University of Kansas. 2001.

My dissertation entitled Cultural Icons in Latin American Theater : Studies of Frida Kahlo Carlos Gardel, Eva Perón and Selena Quintanilla-Pérez demonstrates that the thread that unites these figures is their foundation in art and performance. Although in some cases much has been written about these famous artists, there is surprisingly little research in the area of theater. Through their individual arts (Kahlo's paintings, Gardel and the tango, Evita's career as an actor and Selena's Tex-Mex style music), this study shows how these famous figures fashioned public personae and created roles for themselves that they subsequently performed in everyday life. These performances on stage and in life became layered, and this multidimensionality allows them to continue their popularity even after death. Their art and images have begun to appear everywhere, and in the same way that historical icons came to represent various liturgical texts, these icons of popular culture resurfaced at the end of the twentieth-century as symbols for debate about various discourses circulating in literature, culture, society and politics. Through a performance and cultural studies based approach, this project explores topics as diverse as gender studies, Mexican politics from the Revolution to the 1968 massacre at Tlatelolco, the NAFTA trade agreement, dictatorships in South America, national apathy, immigration, exile, border cultures and Latino(a)/Chicano(a) identity. [Author Abstract]

19.)   **Whitt, E. A.**

Ambiguity and paradox: Re-examining selected paintings by Frida Kahlo.

M.A. thesis, University of Louisville. 2002.

This study will concentrate primarily on six of Kahlo's paintings: *My Birth, A Few Small Nips. Self-Portrait with Cropped Hair, The Little Deer, The Love Embrace of the Universe, the Earth (Mexico), Myself, Diego and Sehor Xolotl,* and *Diego and I.* It follows a roughly chronological pattern that ultimately gives insight into Kahlo's evolution as an artist, wife, and woman. Each chapter revolves around compositional and contextual analysis and around a discussion of the ambiguous and paradoxical nature Kahlo's work. Chapter one will focus on *My Birth* (ill. I), painted in 1932 and *A Few Small Nips* (ill. II), painted in 1935. The two paintings are compared in terms of composition, subject matter, and effect on the viewer. The major question that is addressed is that of whether Kahlo wished to be a mother. It has been argued that much of her work was a reaction to her inability to produce offspring for Rivera. Herrera notes that. "Many of her paintings express this fascination with procreation, and some directly reflect her despair at not having children" (148). The reasons behind this argument are reviewed and refuted. The chapter also discusses the idea of the scripted narrative and how this affected Kahlo's denial of or acceptance of her inability to be a mother. *Self-Portrait with Cropped Hair* (ill. IV). created in 1940, and the 1946 work. *The Little Deer* (ill. V). provide the foundation for chapter two. This chapter again reevaluates Kahlo's work in terms of its composition and continues the discussion of ambiguity and ambivalence found in much of her work. The idea of a scripted narrative for women will be revisited, now with a look into Kahlo's purposeful attack of traditional Mexican values and gendered assumptions. In each of these paintings, she clearly questions the role a woman is expected to play, thereby creating a forum ripe with opportunities to redefine these roles. In the third chapter, *The Love Embrace of the Universe, the Earth (Mexico). Myself Diego and Sehor Xolotl* (ill. VI) and *Diego and I* (ill. VII). both painted in 1949 will be discussed. As with previous chapters, the ways in which composition dictates the message of the works and how ambiguity- and ambivalence present themselves as predominant themes in Kahlo's paintings are examined. The analysis of these two works makes clear not only Kahlo's maturation as an artist, but also her maturation as a wife and as a woman. Here, we see that Kahlo has drawn some conclusions about her own life and about the place women hold in the universe. These paintings comment on race, class, gender, and society as well as on her life. Frida Kahlo, like many women artists, has been misunderstood and taken for granted for decades. This reexamination should open the doors to a new understanding of her art and her life and thereby aid in the

comprehension of motivations of other women artists who are or have been subjected to the scripted narrative prescribed to them by patriarchical systems. [Author Abstract shortened by LV Allene]

20.)   **Zetterman, E. M.**

Frida Kahlos bildspraak: Ansikte, kropp and landskap. Representation av nationell identitet (Frida Kahlo bildspraak: Face, body and landscape. Representation of national identity).

Ph.D. dissertation, Goteborgs University (Sweden). 2003.

This thesis is about the Mexican artist Frida Kahlo (1907-1954) and her works, with emphasis on her painted self-portraits. The objective is to place Frida Kahlo's pictorial production in relation to a place and time specific context and test the theory of Frida Kahlo's self-portraits as a project connected to a general striving towards a new formulation of national identity. The majority of Frida Kahlo's pictorial production coincides with a historically delimited era in which there was a break from earlier role models and ideals, politically, culturally and ideologically. This phase was an artistically dynamic period with a redefining view of art and the history of the nation, a visualisation of the mythology and symbolism of the Indian cultures of origin, and an emphasis on the Indian ethnicity of the nation. Two chapters describe the ideological context in which Frida Kahlo's works were created. The visual markers around which the post-revolutionary national discourse came to revolve are identified and certain concepts related to race are examined. The subsequent chapters are devoted to Frida Kahlo's pictures. One chapter examines how her pictorial production in the 1920's emerged in a dialogue with contemporary art theory. One chapter deals with body thematics based on the naked female body, and elements of sex education are put in relation to an ongoing debate on sex education in Mexican schools. Thereafter new features are explored that are introduced in her self-portraits during the late 1930's and that came to be consistent features in her continued production of self-portraits. In the concluding section of the thesis, the self-portraits are discussed from a more general perspective. Some of the myths upon which earlier biographical interpretations were based are questioned. Instead, the thematics of suffering found in the self-portraits are related to the reconstruction of the nation's ethnic identity and problematic issues based on the 16th century Spanish Conquest of the indigenous Indian population. In her complex imagery, Frida Kahlo refers to a broad spectrum of disparate pictorial traditions, stylistic epochs, categories of motifs and symbolic imagery, and to historical, religious and mythical female personages such as Malintzín, la Chingada, Sor Juana, and the Virgin of Guadalupe. These references from different epochs represent the two fundamental components of Mexico's cultural heritage--the Spanish and the Indian--and these are merged in Frida Kahlo self-portraits so that they thereby communicate a construction of identity based on a national heritage. The time perspective of the discussion reaches backwards to before the Spanish Conquest in the 16th century and forwards to the contemporary Chicana/Chicano movement north of the border to the United States. [Author Abstract]

Locating Dissertations and Theses

A. Purchase

Many of the dissertations and theses listed in this bibliography are available for purchase through UMI Dissertation Express:

http://disexpress.umi.com/dxweb

By Fax:

800-864-0019

By Mail:

789 E. Eisenhower Parkway, P.O. Box 1346, Ann Arbor, Michigan 48106-1346

800-521-3042

B. Interlibrary Loan

Dissertations and theses may also be requested through Interlibrary Loan via your local public, college or university library.

www.ingramcontent.com/pod-product-compliance
Lightning Source LLC
Chambersburg PA
CBHW070943180526
45168CB00003B/1165